First German

AT HOME

Kathy Gemmell and Jenny Tyler
Illustrated by Sue Stitt
Designed by Diane Thistlethwaite

Consultant: Sandy Walker

CONTENTS

First published in 1993 by Usborne Publishing Ltd.
Usborne House, 83-85 Saffron Hill
London EC1N 8RT, England.
Copyright © 1993 Usborne Publishing Ltd.
First published in America August 1993.
Printed in Portugal.
Universal Edition.

Speaking German

This book is about the Strudel family. They are going to help you learn to speak German.

Word lists
You will find a word list on every double page to tell you what the German words mean.

Hallo
hullaw

Word list
Guten Tag	gootn tahg	hello
Hallo	hullaw	hi
nein	nine	no
ja	yah	yes
ich	ikh	I
Tschüß	tshewss	bye!
du bist dran	doo bist dran	your turn

GutenTag
gootn tahg

The little letters are to help you say the German words. Read them as if they were English words.

Ich...
ikh

Tschüß
tshewss

Nein
nine

Ja
yah

The best way to find out how to say German words is to listen to a German person speaking. Some letters and sounds are a bit different from English. Here are some clues to help you.

When you see a "ch" in German, it is written "kh" in the little letters. Say this like the "h" in "huge". Try saying *ich*, which means "I".

Say "sch" like the "sh" sound in "show".

When you see one of these: ß, just say it like a double "s".

To say the ü, round your lips to say "oo" then say "ee" instead.

The letter "j" in German sounds like the English "y".

Try saying out loud what each person on this page is saying.

See if you can find Josefina the mouse on each double page.

Games with word lists
You can play games with the word lists if you like. Here are some ideas.

1. Cover all the German words and see if you can say the German for each English word. Score a point for each one you can remember.

2. Time yourself and see if you can say the whole list more quickly next time.

3. Race a friend. The first one to say the German for each word scores a point. The winner is the one to score the most points.

4. Play all these games the other way around, saying the English for each German word.

Du bist dran
Look for the *du bist dran* boxes in this book. There is something for you to do in each of them. *Du bist dran* means "your turn".

Look out for the joke bubbles on some of the pages.

3

The Strudels

Here the Strudel family are introducing themselves. *Ich heiße* [ikh hyssa] means "I am called" or "my name is".

Bella has chased Josefina through the Strudel's garden. See if you can follow her route from Onkel Helmut to where she is now. Which members of the family did she pass on the way?

Word list

ich heiße ikh hyssa	I am called
Herr hair	Mr.
Frau fraow	Mrs.
Oma awma	Granny
Onkel onkel	uncle
Tante tanta	aunt
Guten Morgen gootn more gn	good morning
Auf Wiedersehen owf veederzane	goodbye

Names

Strudel shtroodel	**Helmut** helmoot
Rainer ryner	**Max** mux
Silvia zilveeya	**Bella** bella
Markus mahrkoos	**Josefina** yawzefeena
Uli oolee	**Franz** frunts
Karin kahrin	**Hans** hunts
Ilse ilza	**Katja** katya

Ich heiße Silvia.

Ich heiße Rainer.

Ich heiße Max.

Ich heiße Uli.

Ich heiße Oma Strudel.

Ich heiße Katja.

Ich heiße Markus.

Good morning

Guten Morgen [gootn more gn] means "good morning". Silvia is so sleepy, she has mixed up everyone's names. Say *Guten Morgen* for her, adding the correct name each time.

Guten Morgen Markus

Guten Morgen Oma

4

Du bist dran

Introduce yourself in German by saying *ich heiße* followed by your name. You can introduce your family and pets, using *er heißt* [air hyste] for males (he is called) and *sie heißt* [zee hyste] for females (she is called).

5

At home

Here is the inside of the Strudel family house. Can you find a way around the house, passing all those who are waiting to tell you the names of the rooms on the way? You must not pass anyone more than once.

Start at the door nearest Frau Strudel and go out by the kitchen door. (Remember that doors are not the only way to get from room to room.)

Bei uns [by oonts] means "at our home". "At my home" is *bei mir* [by meer]. At anyone else's home is *bei* then the name of the person, so "at Silvia's home" would be *bei Silvia* [by zilveeya].

Word list

hier ist *here ist*	here is
das Schlafzimmer *dass shlahf tsimmer*	bedroom
das Badezimmer *dass bahda tsimmer*	bathroom
die Mansarde *dee man sarda*	attic
der Keller *dare keller*	cellar
die Küche *dee kewkha*	kitchen
das Wohnzimmer *dass vawn tsimmer*	lounge
das Eßzimmer *dass ess tsimmer*	dining room
das Haus *dass howss*	house
der Garten *dare gartn*	garden
Mutti *moottee*	mum
bei uns *by oonts*	at our home

7

Draw a map

Silvia and Markus have drawn a map of the area near their house and have written all the names in German.

Draw a map of your own area or somewhere you think you would like to live and label it in German.

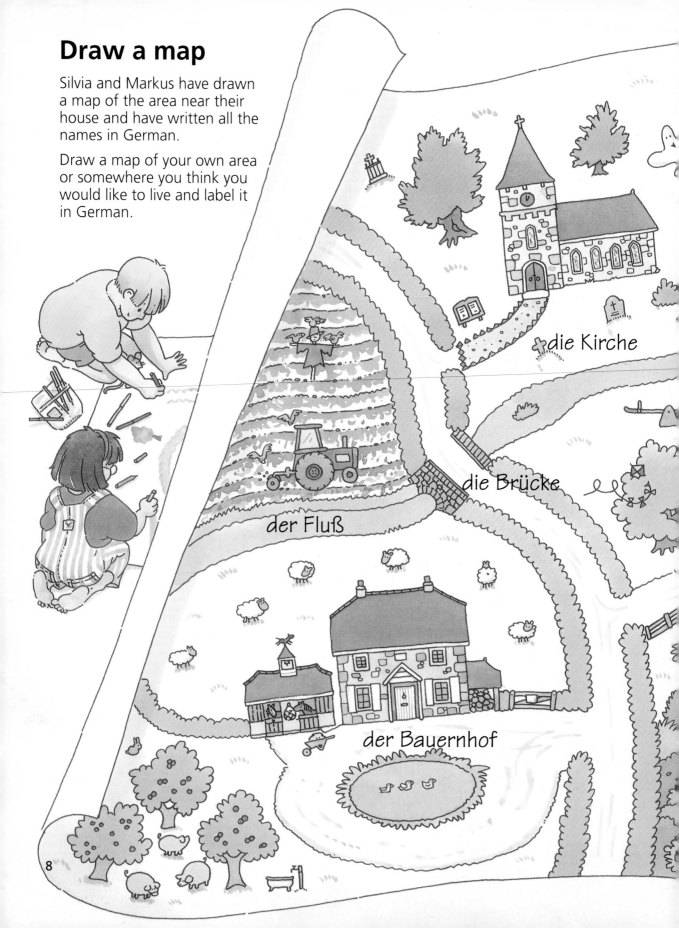

die Kirche

die Brücke

der Fluß

der Bauernhof

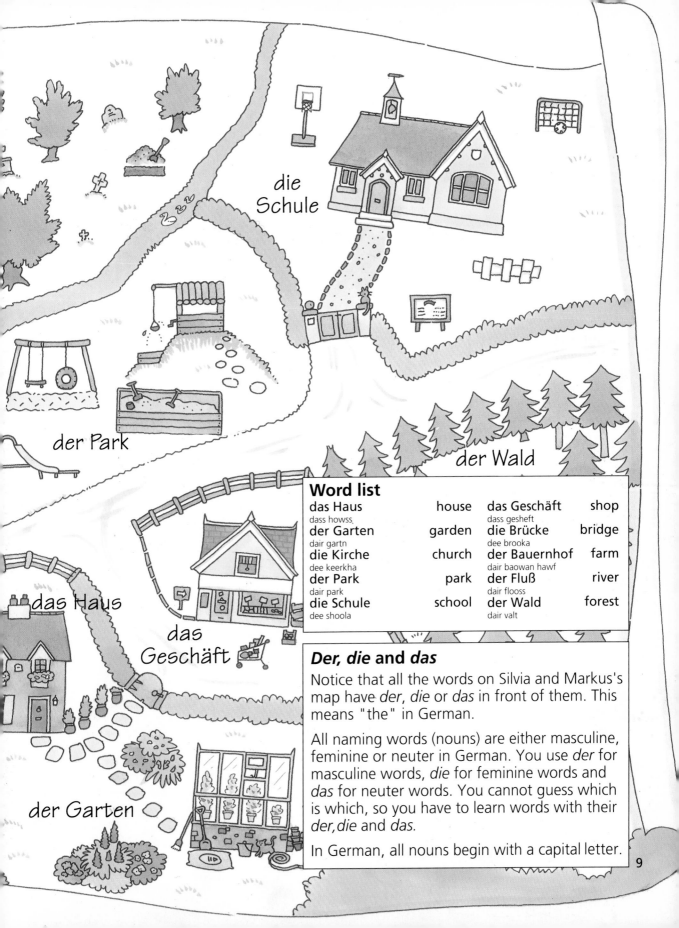

die Schule

der Park

der Wald

das Haus

das Geschäft

der Garten

Word list

das Haus	house	**das Geschäft**	shop
dass howss		dass gesheft	
der Garten	garden	**die Brücke**	bridge
dair gartn		dee brooka	
die Kirche	church	**der Bauernhof**	farm
dee keerkha		dair baowan hawf	
der Park	park	**der Fluß**	river
dair park		dair flooss	
die Schule	school	**der Wald**	forest
dee shoola		dair valt	

Der, die and *das*

Notice that all the words on Silvia and Markus's map have *der*, *die* or *das* in front of them. This means "the" in German.

All naming words (nouns) are either masculine, feminine or neuter in German. You use *der* for masculine words, *die* for feminine words and *das* for neuter words. You cannot guess which is which, so you have to learn words with their *der*, *die* and *das*.

In German, all nouns begin with a capital letter.

Counting in German

Silvia and Markus stayed up late to finish their map and now can't sleep. In fact, everybody is counting things to help them get to sleep.

Count out loud in German for each person. Who do you think fell asleep first? Use the number list to help you.

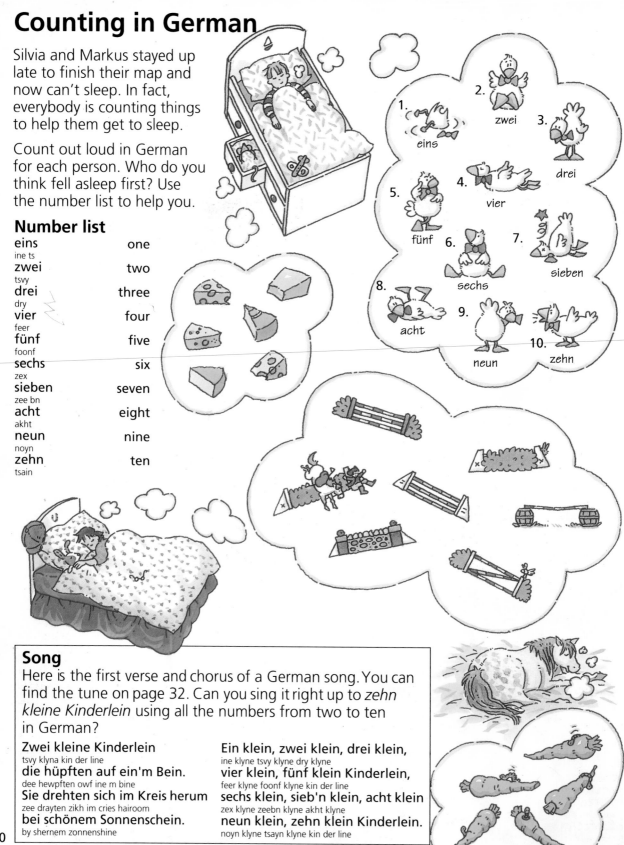

Number list

eins ine ts	one
zwei tsvy	two
drei dry	three
vier feer	four
fünf foonf	five
sechs zex	six
sieben zee bn	seven
acht akht	eight
neun noyn	nine
zehn tsain	ten

1. eins
2. zwei
3. drei
4. vier
5. fünf
6. sechs
7. sieben
8. acht
9. neun
10. zehn

Song

Here is the first verse and chorus of a German song. You can find the tune on page 32. Can you sing it right up to *zehn kleine Kinderlein* using all the numbers from two to ten in German?

Zwei kleine Kinderlein
tsvy klyna kin der line
die hüpften auf ein'm Bein.
dee hewpften owf ine m bine
Sie drehten sich im Kreis herum
zee drayten zikh im cries hairoom
bei schönem Sonnenschein.
by shernem zonnenshine

Ein klein, zwei klein, drei klein,
ine klyne tsvy klyne dry klyne
vier klein, fünf klein Kinderlein
feer klyne foonf klyne kin der line
sechs klein, sieb'n klein, acht klein
zex klyne zeebn klyne akht klyne
neun klein, zehn klein Kinderlein.
noyn klyne tsayn klyne kin der line

10

Note: This is what the song means, "Two little children hopped on one leg. They went around in circles in the lovely sunshine". Chorus: "One little, two little, three little, four little, five little children, six little, seven little, eight little, nine little, ten little children."

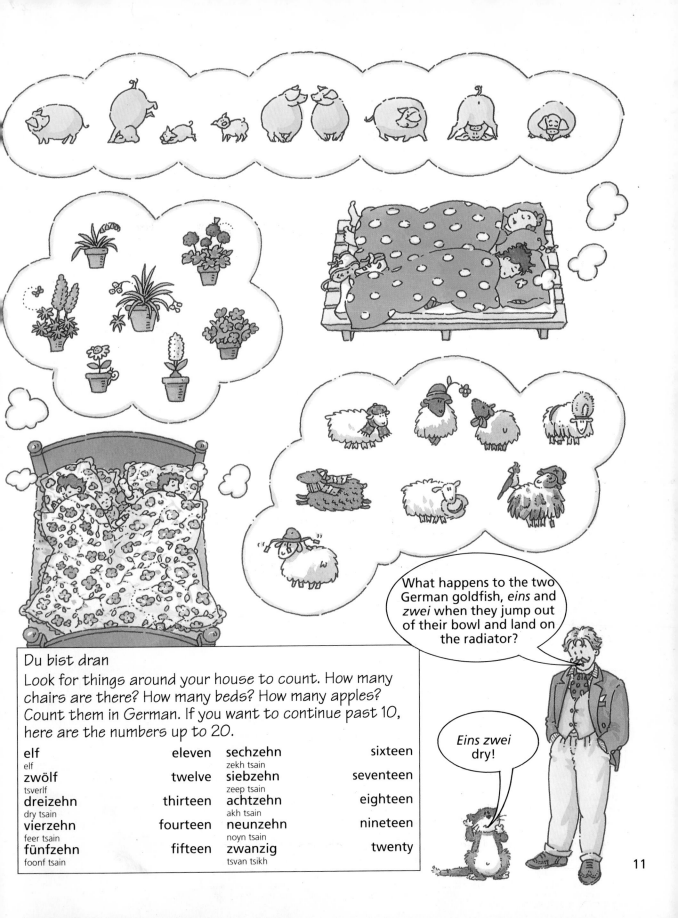

Du bist dran

Look for things around your house to count. How many
chairs are there? How many beds? How many apples?
Count them in German. If you want to continue past 10,
here are the numbers up to 20.

elf elf	eleven	**sechzehn** zekh tsain	sixteen
zwölf tsverlf	twelve	**siebzehn** zeep tsain	seventeen
dreizehn dry tsain	thirteen	**achtzehn** akh tsain	eighteen
vierzehn feer tsain	fourteen	**neunzehn** noyn tsain	nineteen
fünfzehn foonf tsain	fifteen	**zwanzig** tsvan tsikh	twenty

What happens to the two German goldfish, *eins* and *zwei* when they jump out of their bowl and land on the radiator?

Eins zwei dry!

11

Jigsaw puzzles

The next morning everybody is tired and a little bit grumpy. Rainer has brought down some jigsaw puzzles to try and cheer up the family. However, the pieces are all mixed up and Markus is the only one who can see what his puzzle is, *ein Apfel* (an apple).

Can you say in German what all the other puzzles should be? Use the picture list to help you. Only one of the missing pieces cannot be found anywhere. Who will not be able to finish their jigsaw?

Ein, eine and *eins*

In German there are two ways to say "a" something or "one" something, *ein* or *eine*. All *der* and *das* words are *ein* words and all *die* words are *eine* words. To say "one" when you are counting, you say *eins* [ine ts].

Ein Apfel

Picture list

eine Pflaume
ine a pflaow ma
a plum

eine Ananas
ine a ananass
a pineapple

eine Banane
ine a banana
a banana

ein Pfirsich
ine pfeer zikh
a peach

eine Birne
ine a beerna
a pear

eine Apfelsine
ine a apfull zeena
an orange

ein Apfel
ine ap full
an apple

Du bist dran
See if you can remember the words for all these fruits and say what's in your fruit bowl at home.

Answer these questions out loud in German.

Can you see what Josefina is eating? What would Max like to eat?

Song

Here is a song about the fruit and vegetables that Josefina likes and dislikes. Can you guess what any of them are? You can see what all the words mean on page 32.

Kopf–sa–lat und Gur–ke frißt Jo–se–fi–na gern,
kopf za laht oont goor ka frist yaw za fee na gairn

A – ber Blu–men–kohl und Boh–nen nicht so sehr.
ah ber bloo men kawl oont baw nen nikht zaw zair

Sie mag Pam–pel–mu–se, An–an–as und Birn',
zee mahg pum pull moo za an an ass oont beern

A – ber ih–re Erb–sen gibt sie al–le mir.
ah ber ee ra airb sen geept zee al la meer

13

Joke: What's blue and square? An orange in disguise.

What is it?

Oma has ordered lots of new things for her room. They have just been delivered. *Was ist das?* [vass ist dass] means "what is it?" or "what is that?".

Can you help the rest of the family say in German what is in each parcel? Say *das ist* [dass ist] which means "it is" and then the object. Use the picture list to help you with the names.

Remember that *ein* and *eine* both mean "one" or "a".

Picture list

ein Tisch
ine tish
a table

ein Stuhl
ine shtool
a chair

ein Bett
ine bet
a bed

ein Fernseher
ine fairn zayer
a television

eine Vase
ine a vahza
a vase

ein Wecker
ine vecker
an alarm clock

eine Lampe
ine a lampa
a lamp

eine Tasse
ine a tassa
a cup

ein Teller
ine teller
a plate

Du bist dran

Can you find all the things on the picture list in your own house? If you can, point to each one and say what it is in German, using *das ist* [dass ist] and then the name of the object.

Joke: What's this? It's this the other way around.

A day in the life of the Strudels

This is a picture strip of a typical weekend day in the Strudel household - after a good night's sleep this time - but the pictures are all in the wrong order. Can you decide which order they should be in?

Use the word list to help you to say out loud what everyone is saying.

Word list

das Frühstück — breakfast
dass frew shtook
das Mittagessen — lunch
dass mittah gessn
das Abendessen — dinner
dass ah bnd essn
morgens — in the morning
more gns
nachmittags — in the afternoon
nakh mittahks
Guten Morgen — good morning
gootn more gn
Guten Abend — good evening
gootn ah bnd
Gute Nacht — good night
goota nakht
schlaf gut — sleep well
shlahf goot
es ist 3 Uhr — it is three o'clock
ess ist dry oor
es ist 8 Uhr — it is eight o'clock
ess ist akht oor

Here is a little rhyme about Franz. Can you spot him in two of the pictures?

Das kleine Kaninchen
dass klyna ka neen khn
Steht auf um sieben
shtate owf oom zeebn
Abends um acht
ah bnds oom akht
Sagt "gute Nacht".
zahkt goota nakht

You can check what all the words mean on page 32.

Guten Appetit [gootn appa teet] is what you say before eating in Germany. It means "enjoy your meal".

Essen kommen [essn kommn] is how you tell people in German to come and eat.

Afternoon activity

This afternoon the Strudels are all busy doing things in and around the house. Can you find someone doing each of the things on the word list somewhere in the big picture?

As you find each one, read out loud what that person is saying in German.

Word list

ich esse ikh essa	I am eating
ich lese ikh layza	I am reading
ich laufe ikh laowfa	I am running
ich gehe ikh gaya	I am walking
ich singe ikh zinga	I am singing
ich trinke ikh trinka	I am drinking
ich spreche ikh shprekha	I am speaking
ich schlafe ikh shlahfa	I am sleeping
ich arbeite ikh ahr byta	I am working
ich schwimme ikh shvimma	I am swimming
ich falle ikh falla	I am falling
ich gehe aus ikh gaya owss	I am going out
ich springe ikh shpringa	I am jumping

Du bist dran
Was machst du?
[vass makhst doo].
What are you doing at
the moment? You're
probably reading, so you
say *ich lese* [ich layza].
See if you can do all the
other things in the
picture and remember
how to say them
in German.

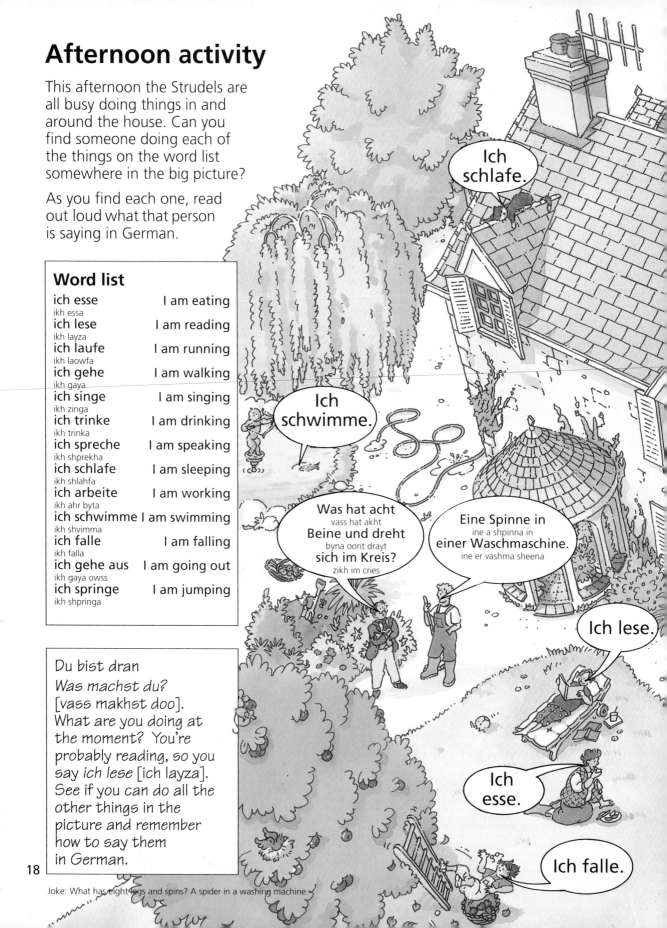

Joke: What has eight legs and spins? A spider in a washing machine.

Happy birthday

The next day is Oma's birthday and the family is having a party for her. There are lots of different kinds of food because everyone likes different things.

To say you like something in German you say *ich mag* [ikh mahg] and then the thing you like. To say you don't like something you say the thing you don't like and then *mag ich nicht* [mahg ikh nikht].

"Happy birthday" in German is *Herzlichen Glückwunsch zum Geburtstag* [hairtslikhn glookvoontsh tsoom gaboorts tahg].

Word list

ich mag ikh mahg	I like
...mag ich nicht mahg ikh nikht	I don't like...
Obst awpst	fruit
Käse kayza	cheese
Brot brawt	bread
Gemüse gamooza	vegetables
Marmelade marmalahda	jam
Pralinen prah leenan	chocolates
Salat zallaht	salad
Schinken shinkan	ham
Suppe zooppa	soup
Pommes frites pom frit	french fries
Torten tortn	cakes
Würstchen verst khen	sausages

Can you see which people do not like the food in front of them? Say out loud in German what they are thinking.

What do you think Silvia is saying? How would Max say what he likes in German?

Du bist dran

Was magst du? [vass mahgst doo] means "what do you like?" Say what you like to eat out loud in German. *Was magst du nicht?* [vass mahgst doo nikht] means "what do you not like?" Can you say what you don't like to eat in German?

In German most cakes are called *Torten* but some sponge cakes are called *Kuchen* [kookhen].

Silvia goes shopping

Today is a school holiday and Silvia has gone to do the shopping.

Can you see from the picture what Silvia is asking for? *Ich möchte* [ikh merkhte] means "I would like" and *und* [oont] means "and".

Now try to ask for all the items on Silvia's shopping list in German. Remember to say "please", *bitte* [bitta] and "thank you", *danke schön* [dunka shern].

Der, *die* and *das* all change to *die* when you are talking about more than one thing. The name of the thing usually changes a bit as well.

Ich möchte eine Zeitung und ein Eis, bitte.

Liste
4 Äpfel
9 Bananen
8 Brötchen
5 Zwiebeln
6 Fische
2 Torten

Can you see from the picture how to say "How much does that come to?" in German? Say it out loud.

What do you think Uli will ask for? Say it for him.

Number reminder

eins ine ts	one	sechs zex	six
zwei tsvy	two	sieben zee bn	seven
drei dry	three	acht akht	eight
vier feer	four	neun noyn	nine
fünf foonf	five	zehn tsain	ten

Du bist dran

Wieviel [vee feel] means "how much" in German and *wieviele* [vee feela] means "how many". Can you answer the following questions by looking at the picture? Use the number reminder to help you count up in German how many there are.

Wieviele Blumen?
Wieviele Hüte?
Wieviele Katzen?

22

Note: The money used in Germany is German Marks, called *Deutschmark* (DM), and *Pfennigs* (Pf). There are 100 Pfennigs to a Mark.

Word list

ich möchte ikh merkhte	I would like
die Katze dee katsa	cat
der Apfel dair apfull	apple
die Banane dee banana	banana
das Brötchen dass brert khen	roll
die Zwiebel dee tsveebel	onion
das macht...Mark dass makht...mark	that's...Mark
wieviel macht das? vee feel makht dass	how much does that come to?
der Fisch dair fish	fish
die Blume dee blooma	flower
die Torte dee torta	cake
das Eis dass ice	ice cream cone
bitte bitta	please
danke schön dunka shern	thank you
der Hut dair hoot	hat
die Zeitung dee tsy toong	newspaper

Joke: Which dogs don't bite? Hot dogs

23

Market day

Later on, the whole family goes down to the market. Everybody in the village seems to be there. It is so crowded that the Strudels have split up and are all doing things in different parts of the market.

Uli asks where Franz is and the butcher points to him. *Wo ist* [vaw ist] means "where is" and *da ist Franz* [dah ist frunts] means "there's Franz".

Can you spot all of the Strudels in the crowd? Point to each one and say *da ist* [dah ist] followed by the person's name.

Wo ist Bella?

Wo ist Max?

Wo ist Josefina?

Wo ist Franz?

Da ist Franz.

Danke schön

Wo gehst
vaw gayst
du hin?
doo hin

Ich ziehe um.
ikh tseeya oom

24

Joke: Where are you going? I'm moving (house).

Dominoes to make

For something to do at home, Silvia and Markus have invented a game of dominoes which uses German colours. Here's how to make one like theirs and play it.

1. Cut your cardboard into 28 rectangles about 8cm long and 4cm wide (3in by 1½in). You can make the rectangles bigger if you have more cardboard.

You will need:
white cardboard (at least 32cm by 28 cm, 13in by 11in), felt tips, scissors and a black pen.

2. Copy the colours and words from the small dominoes shown here onto your rectangles. Use the colour guide to help you.

3. The idea of the game is to fit all the dominoes into a pattern, matching up the colours as shown below. If you are playing by yourself, the double-red starts.

You can place doubles across the line, as shown here.

The domino line can turn corners.

4. You can only add one domino to each colour and you must shout out the name of that colour before you put down your domino.

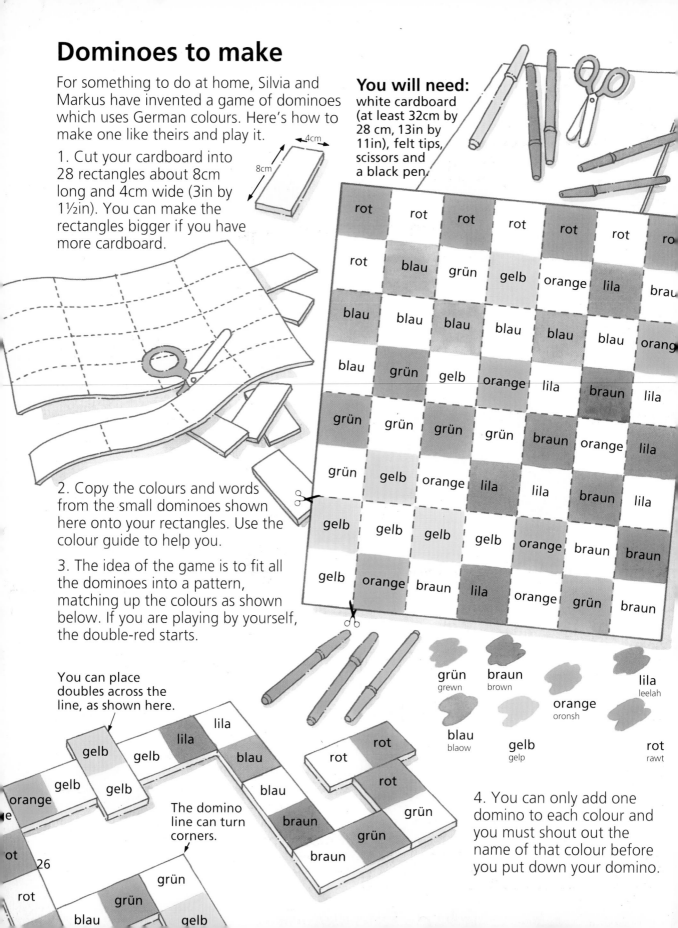

Colour guide:
grün — grewn
braun — brown
lila — leelah
orange — oronsh
blau — blaow
gelb — gelp
rot — rawt

Domino grid colours/words:
rot, rot, rot, rot, rot, rot, ro
rot, blau, grün, gelb, orange, lila, brau
blau, blau, blau, blau, blau, blau, orang
blau, grün, gelb, orange, lila, braun, lila
grün, grün, grün, grün, braun, orange, lila
grün, gelb, orange, lila, lila, braun, lila
gelb, gelb, gelb, gelb, orange, braun, braun
gelb, orange, braun, lila, orange, grün, braun

Example layout words:
lila, lila, blau, gelb, gelb, blau, gelb, gelb, orange, rot, 26, rot, blau, grün, grün, gelb, rot, rot, rot, grün, braun, grün, braun

5. If you are playing with a friend, first spread the dominoes out, face-down, on the table or floor. Take seven dominoes each and put them face-up in front of you. These form your "hand".

6. The idea of this game is to get rid of all the dominoes in your hand and the first person to do so is the winner.

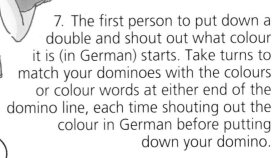

Du bist dran.

7. The first person to put down a double and shout out what colour it is (in German) starts. Take turns to match your dominoes with the colours or colour words at either end of the domino line, each time shouting out the colour in German before putting down your domino.

8. If you can't go, you must pick up a spare domino if there is one left, or miss a turn if there is not.

Word list

du bist dran	your turn
doo bist dran	
ich habe gewonnen	I've won
ikh hahba gavonnen	

Ich habe gewonnen.

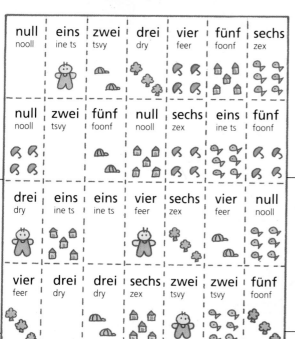

null	eins	zwei	drei	vier	fünf	sechs
nooll	ine ts	tsvy	dry	feer	foonf	zex

null	zwei	fünf	null	sechs	eins	fünf
nooll	tsvy	foonf	nooll	zex	ine ts	foonf

drei	eins	eins	vier	sechs	vier	null
dry	ine ts	ine ts	feer	zex	feer	nooll

vier	drei	drei	sechs	zwei	zwei	fünf
feer	dry	dry	zex	tsvy	tsvy	foonf

Number dominoes

You could also make German number dominoes. Copy these dominoes onto pieces of cardboard (the same as the ones used for Colour dominoes) and play in the same way, this time matching up the number of objects with the number in German. The double-six fish starts.

27

Memory game

Here is a game which you can play again and again. The idea is to get to the finish as quickly as possible.

You will need:

a dice
a clock or watch

How to play

Look at the time when you start. Throw the dice and count with your finger the number of squares shown on the dice. Say the answer to the question on that square out loud then shake again.

If you land on a square with no question on it, shake again and move on.

All the answers can be found in this book, so if you can't remember or are not sure, look through the book until you find the correct answer.

Look at the time again when you finish. Can you do it more quickly next time?

Which way would you say *die Kirche*?

1.dye keerkha
2.dee keerkha
3.dee kersha

Tell Markus how to ask for an ice cream cone in German.

Wieviele Blumen?

Say "yes" in German.

Say "hi" i German.

What would Markus say if you asked, Was machst du?

Was ist das?

How do you introduce yourself in German?

1.rot
2.lila
3.gelb

Say "hello" in German.

Which of these describes Katja's balloon?

What is Silvia saying to Herr Grün?

Say "good night" in German.

Which of these is Silvia saying?

Say "I am eating" in German.

1.Ich mag Käse
2.Ich mag Schinken
3.Ich mag Pralinen

How will Markus tell his friend what Josefina's name is?

Start
shtart
(start)

28

Word list

Here is a list of all the German words and phrases used in this book in alphabetical order. You can use the list either to check quickly what a word means, or to test yourself. Cover up any German or English word or phrase and see if you can say its translation. (Remember that some words change slightly when you are talking about more than one thing.)

Abendessen (das)	ah bnd essn	dinner
abends	ah bnds	in the evening
aber	ah ber	but
acht	akht	eight
achtzehn	akh tsain	eighteen
Ananas (die)	ananass	pineapple
Apfel (der)	ap full	apple
Äpfel (die)	ep full	apples
Apfelsine (die)	ap full zeena	orange
Auf Wiedersehen	owf veederzane	goodbye
Badezimmer (das)	bahda tsimmer	bathroom
Banane (die)	banana	banana
Bauernhof (der)	baowan hawf	farm
bei mir	by meer	at my home
Bein (das)	bine	leg
Bett (das)	bet	bed
Birne (die)	beerna	pear
bitte	bitta	please
blau	blaow	blue
Blume (die)	blooma	flower
Blumenkohl (der)	bloo men kawl	cauliflower
Bohnen (die)	baw nen	beans
braun	brown	brown
Brot (das)	brawt	bread
Brötchen (das)	brert khen	roll
Brücke (die)	brooka*	bridge
da ist (Franz)	dah ist (frunts)	there's (Franz)
danke schön	dunka shern	thank you very much
das ist	dass ist	it/that is
das macht...Mark	dass makht..mark	that makes...Marks
der, die, das	dair, dee, dass	the
drei	dry	three
dreizehn	dry tsain	thirteen
du bist dran	doo bist dran	your turn
ein, eine	ine, ine a	a/an/one
eins	ine ts	one
Eis (das)	ice	ice cream cone
elf	elf	eleven
er	air	he
er dreht sich	air drayt zikh	he spins
er heißt	air hyste	he is called

er sagt	air zahkt	he says
er steht auf	air shtate owf	he gets up
Erbsen (die)	airb sen	peas
es	ess	it
es ist ...Uhr	ess ist...oor	it is...o'clock
essen kommen	essn kommn	come and eat
Eßzimmer (das)	ess tsimmer	dining room
Fernseher (der)	fairn zayer	television
Fisch (der)	fish	fish
Fluß (der)	flooss*	river
Frau	fraow	Mrs.
Frühstück (das)	frew shtook*	breakfast
fünf	foonf*	five
fünfzehn	foonf tsain*	fifteen
Garten (der)	gartn	garden
gelb	gelp	yellow
Gemüse (das)	gamooza	vegetables
Geschäft (das)	gesheft	shop
grün	grewn	green
Gurke (die)	goorka	cucumber
Guten Abend	gootn ah bnd	good evening
Guten Appetit	gootn appateet	enjoy your meal
Guten Morgen	gootn more gn	good morning
Gute Nacht	goota nakht	good night
Guten Tag	gootn tahg	hello
Hallo	hullaw	hi
Haus (das)	howss	house
Herr	hair	Mr.
Herzlichen Glückwunsch zum Geburtstag	hairtslikhn glookvoontsh* tsoom* gaboorts tahg	happy birthday
hier ist	here ist	here is
Hund (der)	hoont*	dog
Hut (der)	hoot	hat
ich	ikh	I
ich arbeite	ikh ahr byta	I am working
ich esse	ikh essa	I am eating
ich falle	ikh falla	I am falling
ich gehe	ikh gaya	I am walking
ich gehe aus	ikh gaya owss	I am going out
ich habe gewonnen	ikh hahba gavonnen	I've won
ich heiße	ikh hyssa	I am called
ich laufe	ikh laowfa	I am running
ich lese	ikh layza	I am reading
ich mag	ikh mahg	I like
ich möchte	ikh merkhta	I would like
ich schlafe	ikh shlahfa	I am sleeping
ich schwimme	ikh shvimma	I am swimming
ich singe	ikh zinga	I am singing

30

*The 'oo' sound in these words is like the 'u' in 'put'.

ich spreche	ikh shprekha	I am speaking	**sechzehn**	zekh tsain	sixteen
ich springe	ikh shpringa	I am jumping	**sie**	zee	she
ich trinke	ikh trinka	I am drinking	**sieben**	zeebn	seven
ich ziehe um	ikh tseeya oom*	I am moving (house)	**siebzehn**	zeep tsain	seventeen
			sie heißt	zee hyste	she is called
im Kreis	im cries	in a circle	**Spinne (die)**	shpinna	spider
			Start	shtart	start
ja	yah	yes	**Stuhl (der)**	shtool	chair
			Suppe (die)	zooppa*	soup
Kaninchen (das)	ka neen khn	rabbit			
Käse (der)	kayza	cheese	**Tante (die)**	tanta	aunt
Katze (die)	katsa	cat	**Tasse (die)**	tassa	cup
Keller (der)	keller	cellar	**Teller (der)**	teller	plate
Kirche (die)	keerkha	church	**Tisch (der)**	tish	table
kleine	klyna	little	**Torte (die)**	torta	cake
Kopfsalat (der)	kopf za laht	lettuce	**Tschüß**	tshewss	bye
Küche (die)	kewkha	kitchen			
			um	oom*	at
Lampe (die)	lampa	lamp	**umgekehrt**	oom gekairt*	the other way around
lila	leelah	purple	**und**	oont*	and
Liste (die)	lissta	list			
			Vase (die)	vahza	vase
mag ich nicht	mahg ikh nikht	I don't like	**Vati**	fahtee	dad
Mansarde (die)	man sarda	attic	**verkleidete**	fairklydet a	in disguise
Marmelade (die)	marmalahda	jam	**vier**	feer	four
Mittagessen (das)	mittah gessn	lunch	**viereckig**	feer eckig	square
morgens	more gns	in the morning	**vierzehn**	feer tsain	fourteen
Mutti	moottee*	mum			
			Wald (der)	valt	wood
nachmittags	nakh mittahks	in the afternoon	**was ist das?**	vass ist dass	what is it/that?
nein	nine	no	**was machst du?**	vass makhst doo	what are you doing?
neun	noyn	nine	**was magst du?**	vass mahgst doo	what do you like?
neunzehn	noyn tsain	nineteen	**was magst du nicht?**	vass mahgst doo nicht	what do you not like?
null	nooll*	zero	**Waschmaschine (die)**	vashma sheena	washing machine
Obst (das)	awpst	fruit	**Wecker (der)**	vecker	alarm clock
Oma (die)	awma	grandma	**welche..?**	vellkha	which..?
Onkel (der)	onkel	uncle	**wieviele?**	vee feela	how many?
orange	oronsh	orange	**wieviel macht das?**	vee feel makht dass	how much does that come to?
Pampelmuse (die)	pum pull mooza	grapefruit	**wo gehst du hin?**	vaw gayst doo hin	where are you going?
Park (der)	park	park	**Wohnzimmer (das)**	vawn tsimmer	living room
Pfirsich (der)	pfeer zikh	peach	**wo ist..?**	vaw ist	where is..?
Pflaume (die)	pflaow ma	plum	**Würstchen (das)**	verst khen	sausage
Pralinen (die)	prah leenan	chocolates			
Pommes frites (die)	pom frit	french fries	**zehn**	tsain	ten
			Zeitung (die)	tsy toong*	newspaper
rot	rawt	red	**Ziel**	tseel	end
			zwanzig	tsvan tsikh	twenty
Salat (der)	zallaht	salad	**zwei**	tsvy	two
schlaf gut	shlahf goot	sleep well	**Zwiebel (die)**	tsveebel	onion
Schlafzimmer (das)	shlahf tsimmer	bedroom	**zwölf**	tsverlf	twelve
Schinken (der)	shinkan	ham			
Schule (die)	shoola	school			
sechs	zex	six			

Answers

PAGE 4-5

Bella passed *Onkel Helmut, Herr Strudel, Franz, Tante Ilse, Uli, Rainer, Silvia, Max, Katja, Markus, Oma* and *Frau Strudel*.

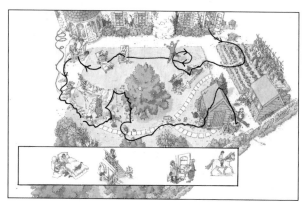

Silvia should say *Guten Morgen Bella, Guten Morgen Markus* and *Guten Morgen Oma*.

PAGE 6-7

This is the way you must go:

PAGE 10-11

Max fell asleep first - he only counted to five before falling asleep. The tune for the song is:

Zwei klei-ne Kin-der-lein die hüpf-ten auf ein'm Bein. Sie
tsvy kly na kin der line dee hewpf ten owf ine m bine zee

dreh-ten sich im Kreis her-um bei schö-nem Sonn-en - schein.
dray ten zikh im cries hair oom by sher nem zonn en shine

Refrain

Ein klein, zwei klein, drei klein, vier klein, fünf klein Kin - der - lein,
ine klyne tsvy klyne dry klyne feer klyne foonf klyne kin der line

Sechs klein, sieb'n klein, acht klein, neun klein, zehn klein Kin-der - lein.
zex klyne zeebn klyne akht klyne noyn klyne tsayn klyne kin der line

PAGE 12-13

What everyone's jigsaws were:
- Herr Strudel-*ein Pfirsich* (a peach),
- Tante Ilse-*eine Birne* (a pear),
- Karin-*eine Banane* (a banana),
- Katja-*eine Ananas* (a pineapple),
- Uli-*eine Pflaume* (a plum),
- Silvia-*eine Apfelsine* (an orange).

Herr Strudel will not be able to finish his jigsaw.

The answers to the questions are:
- Josefina - *eine Pflaume* (a plum),
- Max - *ein Apfel* (an apple).

Here is what the words of the song mean in English
Josefina likes eating
Lettuce and cucumber,
But she doesn't like
Cauliflower and beans much.
She likes grapefruit,
Pineapple and pear,
But all her peas,
She gives to me.

PAGE 16-17

The right order for the pictures is: D F G H B E C A

Here is the rhyme in English:
The little rabbit
Gets up at seven,
In the evening at eight
(He) says "goodnight".

PAGE 20-21

Markus is thinking *Käse mag ich nicht*.
Rainer is thing *Suppe mag ich nicht*.
Onkel Helmut is thinking *Würstchen mag ich nicht*.
Silvia is saying *Ich mag Pommes frites*.
Max would say *Ich mag Obst*.

PAGE 22-23

Silvia is asking for a newspaper and an ice cream cone.

"How much is it?" is *wieviel macht das?*

Uli is going to say *Ich möchte ein Eis, bitte*.

There are:
- 9 *Blumen*
- 5 *Hüte*
- 6 *Katzen*